Charming Lies:

Unmasking the Sociopaths Among Us

Mark Winters

Charming Lies: Unmasking the Sociopaths Among Us

Author Mark Winters

Published By Neil McKenzie

ISBN 9781326920364
Imprint: Lulu.com

Introduction:

The Prevalence of Sociopaths

Research in psychology has long been fascinated by the prevalence of sociopaths in society. Experts estimate that sociopaths, individuals diagnosed with antisocial personality disorder (ASPD), make up between 1% and 4% of the population. While this percentage may appear small, the implications of such a figure are profound. To put it in perspective, in a town of 100 people, at least one person may have a sociopathic personality. In a city of a million, that's potentially 10,000 sociopaths moving undetected in day-to-day life. The numbers scale to a staggering level globally.

The term "sociopath" conjures up images of notorious criminals, violent offenders, and figures on the extreme ends of antisocial behaviour. Popular media is rife with portrayals of sociopaths as inherently dangerous, often highlighting figures who commit crimes of a brutal or violent nature. However, this portrayal fails to capture the nuanced and often subtle ways in which sociopaths actually exist among us. Most sociopaths are not violent criminals lurking in dark alleys; rather, they are far more likely to be the colleague who cuts corners, the neighbour who manipulates others for personal gain, or even a close friend or partner who shows a marked lack of empathy.

In fact, much of the confusion surrounding sociopathy comes from a failure to distinguish between the extreme outliers and the more common cases that present in less dramatic, though no less harmful, ways. The Diagnostic and Statistical Manual of Mental Disorders (DSM-5) defines sociopathy through a range of behaviours, including persistent disregard for others' rights, lack of empathy, chronic dishonesty, and manipulative tendencies. Yet, many sociopaths are adept at concealing these traits behind a veneer of normalcy, even charisma. This ability to mask their true selves makes them particularly dangerous, as they can manipulate and deceive without raising the alarm bells we might expect when we think of someone with such a disorder.

Sociopaths often do not see themselves as having a problem. To them, their behaviours—whether they involve lying, manipulating, or exploiting others—are simply tools to achieve their goals. They lack the moral compass that would prevent someone else from engaging in such behaviours. Without the internal restraints of guilt, remorse, or empathy, they move through the world without concern for the impact their actions have on others. This makes their behaviour difficult to challenge; they do not respond to moral reasoning or emotional appeals the way others might.

The disconnect between the violent stereotype of a sociopath and the more subtle, yet equally damaging, reality is a large part of why so many sociopaths go undetected. They are not always the serial killers or hardened criminals portrayed in media. Many live functional, even successful, lives, occupying roles of power in companies, organisations, or communities. Their manipulative abilities make them particularly adept at climbing social and professional ladders, often leaving a trail of emotional and psychological damage behind them. Because they are not easily identified, they can wreak havoc without ever facing consequences.

Understanding the prevalence of sociopaths and the variety of forms their behaviour can take is crucial in today's world. In personal relationships, professional environments, and even within families, sociopaths can operate under the radar, causing harm while remaining undetected. Their behaviours often go unchallenged because they play on people's trust, empathy, and belief that others operate by the same moral code. Unfortunately, once a person is entangled in a sociopath's web, the consequences can be devastating—emotionally, financially, and psychologically.

Consider the case of "John," a successful business executive who seemed to have it all. He was charming, well-liked by his colleagues, and always seemed to know the right thing to say. But underneath this façade was a ruthless individual who exploited others to get ahead. John used his charm to manipulate coworkers, take credit for others' work, and deceive clients, all while maintaining the appearance of a charismatic leader. By the time his colleagues realised the extent of his manipulation, the damage had been done—careers had been ruined, trust had been broken, and the company had suffered financially.

Stories like John's are not uncommon. Sociopaths can thrive in environments that reward ambition, charisma, and confidence—traits that are often confused with leadership and success. This is why understanding the traits of sociopaths is so important, not just for individuals seeking to protect themselves, but for society at large. Without this understanding, we leave ourselves vulnerable to manipulation and exploitation at the hands of those who lack empathy and regard for others.

Your Purpose

The purpose of this book goes beyond simply explaining who sociopaths are. While understanding the traits and behaviours that define sociopathy is crucial, this book's aim is to empower you, the reader, to recognise and protect yourself from these individuals. Knowledge, in this case, is not just power—it is protection.

Sociopaths are skilled manipulators. They thrive on the ignorance of their targets, using deception, charm, and lies to weave their way into the lives of others. Too often, by the time someone realises they are dealing with a sociopath, it is too late—the emotional, financial, or psychological damage has already been done. This book is about changing that narrative, giving you the tools and insights needed to identify sociopathic behaviour before it has the chance to cause harm.

Perhaps you have already encountered a sociopath in your life. You may have felt manipulated, confused, or emotionally drained without fully understanding why. This book will help you piece together those experiences and provide clarity on how sociopaths operate. More importantly, it will guide you through the process of healing from that exposure, helping you rebuild your emotional and psychological well-being.

If you have never encountered a sociopath—or are unsure if you have—this book will equip you with the ability to recognise the subtle signs that often go unnoticed. Sociopaths rarely announce themselves with obvious antisocial behaviours. Instead, they rely on more covert methods of manipulation, often using charm, flattery, and calculated deceit to gain the trust of their victims. By the time the truth comes to light, the damage is often significant, leaving victims feeling isolated and unsure of whom to trust.

The goal of this book is to help you avoid falling into the traps set by sociopaths. It will teach you to trust your instincts, recognise red flags, and take proactive steps to protect yourself in both personal and professional settings. Whether you are entering a new relationship, navigating a workplace dynamic, or even interacting with someone in your family, the information in this book will serve as a guide to keeping yourself safe from the manipulative behaviours of sociopaths.

In addition to helping, you avoid sociopathic manipulation; this book also aims to empower those who have already been affected by a sociopath. The psychological toll of dealing with a sociopath can be immense. Victims often struggle with feelings of self-doubt, guilt, and confusion. This book will help you understand that the fault does not lie with you. It will offer practical strategies for healing and moving forward, allowing you to rebuild your sense of trust and confidence.

What Readers Will Gain

By the end of this book, you will have gained a comprehensive understanding of sociopathic behaviour and the skills necessary to protect yourself from it. Specifically, you will learn how to:

- Spot the subtle behaviours that sociopaths use to manipulate others: While sociopaths often avoid outright violence or overtly antisocial behaviours, they rely on a set of tactics that can be identified if you know what to look for. These include charm, deception, gaslighting, and emotional manipulation. You will learn to recognise these tactics before they take root, allowing you to protect yourself from further harm.

- Protect yourself in personal and professional environments: Sociopaths are not confined to any one area of life. They can be found in personal relationships, workplaces, social circles, and even within families. This book will teach you how to set boundaries, trust your instincts, and avoid becoming ensnared in their manipulative webs. Whether it's a new relationship, a friendship, or a work dynamic, you'll learn to spot the red flags and protect yourself from sociopathic influence.

- Heal from exposure to a sociopath: If you have already experienced the emotional and psychological toll of dealing with a sociopath, this book will guide you through the healing process. You will learn how to rebuild your confidence, trust, and sense of self after being manipulated or harmed by a sociopath. Recovery is possible, and this book will offer you the tools to move forward with strength and resilience.

Sociopaths are experts at blending in. Their ability to mask their true selves behind a facade of charm and normalcy makes them difficult to detect. However, with the right knowledge and understanding, you can learn to spot the signs, protect yourself from manipulation, and heal from the harm they may cause.

By understanding the nature of sociopaths, you are taking the first step toward safeguarding your emotional and psychological well-being. You are also empowering yourself to navigate life with a greater sense of awareness and confidence, equipped with the tools necessary to avoid falling prey to those who lack empathy and moral conscience.

Chapter 1:

What is Sociopathy?

Sociopathy, a term often used interchangeably with antisocial personality disorder (ASPD), conjures up images of violent criminals, ruthless manipulators, and those devoid of empathy. Yet, the reality of sociopathy is far more complex. It encompasses a spectrum of behaviours and traits that affect not only the individual but also those around them. In this chapter, we'll delve into the clinical definition of sociopathy, explore the debate between psychopathy and sociopathy, and discuss the often-overlooked concept of the "functioning sociopath."

The Psychological Definition

At its core, sociopathy is recognised as a personality disorder under the diagnostic criteria for antisocial personality disorder (ASPD), a clinical diagnosis included in the Diagnostic and Statistical Manual of Mental Disorders, Fifth Edition (DSM-5). The term "sociopath" is not a formal diagnosis but is commonly used to describe individuals who exhibit the traits of ASPD, particularly those who manipulate, deceive, and exploit others without a sense of guilt or remorse. These individuals display a pervasive pattern of disregard for the rights of others, and this behaviour often begins in childhood or early adolescence and continues into adulthood.

The DSM-5 outlines specific criteria for diagnosing ASPD, emphasising a variety of traits and behaviours. A diagnosis of ASPD requires that an individual meet several key criteria:

1. Disregard for Others' Rights: Individuals with ASPD frequently violate the rights of others. This can manifest in harmful behaviours ranging from deceit and manipulation to outright aggression. They may exploit people for personal gain, whether emotionally, financially, or socially.

2. Violation of Social Norms: Sociopaths consistently disregard social rules, often committing acts that violate societal expectations. This can include both minor

infractions, such as dishonesty, and more serious acts like criminal behaviour.

3. Deceitfulness: Lying, conning, and using aliases are hallmarks of ASPD. Sociopaths will often manipulate others to achieve their goals, using deceit as a tool to control and exploit. Their dishonesty is not confined to "small lies" but often involves elaborate schemes designed to benefit themselves at the expense of others.

4. Impulsivity and Failure to Plan Ahead: Sociopaths often act without thinking about the consequences. They may make impulsive decisions that benefit them in the short term but cause long-term harm to others. This impulsivity can extend to various aspects of life, including finances, relationships, and career decisions.

5. Irritability and Aggressiveness: Many individuals with ASPD display irritability and aggression, which can result in physical fights or verbal altercations. Their inability to control their temper often leads to strained relationships and conflict with others.

6. Reckless Disregard for Safety: Sociopaths tend to act recklessly, putting both themselves and others at risk. This could include dangerous driving, substance abuse, or other behaviours that show a lack of concern for safety.

7. Consistent Irresponsibility: Whether in their professional or personal lives, sociopaths frequently fail to fulfil obligations. This can manifest as job instability, financial irresponsibility, or failure to meet family commitments.

8. Lack of Remorse: Perhaps one of the most striking traits of sociopathy is the absence of guilt or remorse. When they harm others, sociopaths rarely feel regret or acknowledge the pain they've caused. Instead, they may rationalise their actions, blame their victims, or simply move on without a second thought.

To meet the criteria for ASPD, these behaviours must not be isolated incidents; they must represent a consistent pattern that persists over time. Furthermore, the DSM-5 specifies that this pattern of behaviour must have begun before the age of 15, though a formal diagnosis is generally not made until adulthood. This developmental trajectory indicates that sociopathy often has deep roots in childhood, with early signs such as cruelty to animals, truancy, theft, or other forms of juvenile delinquency.

While sociopathy is a recognised psychological disorder, it's important to remember that it exists on a spectrum. Some individuals may display only a few traits, while others fully embody the criteria for ASPD. Regardless of where they fall on this spectrum, sociopaths share a common disregard for the welfare of others and a tendency to manipulate, deceive, and exploit those around them.

Differentiating Sociopathy and Psychopathy

One of the most common points of confusion when discussing sociopathy is the distinction between sociopathy and psychopathy. These two terms are often used interchangeably, but they refer to different points on the same antisocial spectrum. Both sociopaths and psychopaths exhibit behaviours associated with antisocial personality disorder, but there are subtle, yet significant, differences between the two.

Psychopathy is often considered a more severe form of sociopathy, characterised by a more calculated and predatory approach to manipulation. Psychopaths are often seen as more controlled, cold, and methodical in their behaviour, whereas sociopaths tend to be more impulsive and erratic. The distinction between these two terms has long been debated by psychologists, with some arguing that psychopathy should be viewed as a separate disorder, while others see it as a more extreme variant of ASPD.

Psychopathy vs. Sociopathy: A Clinical Comparison

One of the key differences between psychopathy and sociopathy lies in empathy. While sociopaths typically have a limited capacity for empathy, psychopaths are often described as completely lacking it. Psychopaths are capable of mimicking emotions, allowing them to deceive others with ease, but they do not actually experience these emotions themselves. This is one reason why psychopaths are often more dangerous than sociopaths; their complete emotional detachment makes them capable of committing acts of cruelty without any emotional interference.

Another key difference lies in emotional regulation. Sociopaths are generally more prone to emotional outbursts and impulsive behaviour. They may act on impulse, driven by anger or frustration, which can lead to violence or reckless decision-making. Psychopaths, on the other hand, are far more calculated and controlled in their actions. They often meticulously plan their behaviour, manipulating others with precision and avoiding the emotional volatility seen in sociopaths.

In the world of criminology, psychopaths are often associated with more severe and predatory behaviour, including violent crime. Studies have shown that a significant percentage of violent offenders exhibit psychopathic traits. However, it's important to note that not all psychopaths are violent, and many are able to function in society without drawing attention to their disorder.

The debate over the distinction between sociopathy and psychopathy also touches on the concept of innate vs. environmental factors. Many psychologists believe that psychopathy is more closely linked to biological and genetic factors, while sociopathy is more often shaped by environmental influences, such as trauma, abuse, or neglect in early childhood. This is why some people differentiate between the "born" psychopath and the "made" sociopath. However, this distinction is not universally accepted, and both genetic and environmental factors likely contribute to the development of each disorder.

Despite the differences, both sociopathy and psychopathy share the common threads of manipulation, deceit, and a lack of empathy. Whether they act impulsively or with cold calculation, both sociopaths and psychopaths leave a trail of emotional and psychological damage in their wake.

The "Functioning" Sociopath

When people think of sociopaths, they often imagine individuals who are constantly in trouble with the law—violent criminals, con artists, or scheming villains. However, this stereotype fails to capture the reality that many sociopaths are what could be described as "functioning sociopaths". These individuals may never commit a crime or engage in overtly antisocial behaviour. Instead, they blend seamlessly into society, holding down jobs, maintaining relationships, and appearing to live relatively normal lives. Beneath this façade, however, they continue to exploit and manipulate others for personal gain.

The term "functioning sociopath" refers to individuals who meet the criteria for ASPD but are able to operate successfully in society. They may hold positions of power in their careers, thrive in social settings, and even maintain long-term relationships. However, their success often comes at the expense of others, as they use manipulation, deceit, and exploitation to get ahead.

How Do Functioning Sociopaths Blend In?

One of the most dangerous aspects of the functioning sociopath is their ability to blend in. Unlike more overt sociopaths who engage in criminal behaviour or extreme antisocial acts, functioning sociopaths use their charm, intelligence, and social skills to mask their true nature. They often present themselves as likeable, charismatic individuals, making it difficult for others to see through their manipulative tendencies.

Functioning sociopaths excel in environments where power, success, and competition are valued. They are often drawn to careers in politics, business, law, and other fields where manipulation and ruthlessness can be disguised as ambition. In these settings, their lack of empathy and moral restraint gives them an advantage over others who are bound by ethical considerations.

For example, a functioning sociopath in the workplace may use subtle manipulation to undermine colleagues, take credit for others' work, or sabotage their competitors. They may engage in unethical business practices, all while maintaining an outward appearance of professionalism and competence. Because they are adept at hiding their true motives, they are often able to rise to positions of power without being exposed for the sociopathic traits that drive their behaviour.

Relationships with a Functioning Sociopath

Functioning sociopaths are also capable of maintaining long-term relationships, though these relationships are typically marked by manipulation, deceit, and a lack of emotional depth. They may enter relationships for personal gain—whether financial, social, or emotional— and use their charm to keep their partners emotionally attached. However, they are unlikely to feel genuine love, empathy, or connection.

In personal relationships, functioning sociopaths may engage in behaviours such as gaslighting, a form of manipulation in which they make their partners question their own perceptions and reality. They may lie, cheat, or manipulate their partners, all while maintaining the appearance of being loving or caring. This can leave their partners feeling confused, emotionally drained, and unsure of what went wrong.

The key to understanding functioning sociopaths is recognising that their ability to blend in does not negate the harm they cause. While they may not engage in overt criminal behaviour, their manipulation and deceit can have devastating emotional, psychological, and even financial consequences for those around them.

Sociopathy vs. Narcissism

Another important distinction to make when discussing sociopathy is the difference between sociopathy and narcissism, or more specifically, narcissistic personality disorder (NPD). Both sociopaths and narcissists exhibit a lack of empathy and a tendency to exploit others, but the motivations and behaviours associated with each disorder differ in key ways.

Narcissistic Personality Disorder is characterised by an inflated sense of self-importance, a deep need for admiration, and a lack of empathy for others. Narcissists are often obsessed with their status, appearance, and how others perceive them. While sociopaths and narcissists share a disregard for others' feelings, the narcissist's primary motivation is often related to their own ego and self-image, whereas the sociopath is driven more by power and control.

Key Differences Between Sociopathy and Narcissism

One of the most significant differences between sociopathy and narcissism is the way each disorder manifests in relationships. While sociopaths are primarily focused on manipulating others for personal gain, narcissists are often more concerned with maintaining their own image and receiving admiration. They may exploit others to feed their egos, but their actions are typically driven by a desire for validation rather than a desire for power or control.

Additionally, while sociopaths are often impulsive and erratic in their behaviour, narcissists tend to be more concerned with how their actions will reflect on them. They are more likely to be strategic in their manipulation, as they are deeply invested in maintaining a positive image in the eyes of others.

Despite these differences, there is significant overlap between sociopathy and narcissism, particularly in their shared lack of empathy and exploitative behaviours. Some individuals may exhibit traits of both disorders, making it difficult to distinguish between them.

However, understanding the differences can help clarify the motivations behind each disorder's behaviour.

Conclusion

Sociopathy is a complex and multifaceted disorder that exists on a spectrum, ranging from the violent and criminal to the charming and manipulative. By understanding the traits and behaviours associated with antisocial personality disorder, as well as the differences between sociopathy, psychopathy, and narcissism, we can better identify these individuals in our lives and protect ourselves from their harmful influence.

In the next chapter, we will explore the root causes of sociopathy, examining both genetic and environmental factors that contribute to the development of this disorder. By understanding where sociopathy comes from, we can gain further insight into how to recognise and avoid those who exhibit its traits.

Chapter 2:

The Mask of Charm

Sociopaths are often thought of as callous, cruel individuals who have little regard for the feelings of others. But what makes them especially dangerous is their ability to mask their true nature behind a façade of charm. The functioning sociopath, in particular, uses charm as a tool to manipulate and control others, blending into society while exploiting those around them. This charm is not a natural, genuine expression of warmth or kindness but rather a learned behaviour designed to deceive and disarm. In this chapter, we will explore the mask of charm that many sociopaths wear, delving into the ways they use superficial relationships, fake emotions, and first impressions to manipulate those around them.

The Charming Exterior

At first glance, a functioning sociopath can seem like an ideal friend, partner, or colleague. They are often charming, witty, and engaging, with an ability to put others at ease. This charm allows them to navigate social situations effortlessly, building a network of acquaintances who view them as likeable, charismatic individuals. However, beneath this charming exterior lies a much darker reality.

The charm of a sociopath is not an inherent personality trait but a carefully cultivated skill. Sociopaths understand that to get what they want—whether it's power, money, or control—they must first win people over. They learn from an early age how to manipulate others by being charming and likeable, often studying the social cues that elicit positive responses from others. Through practice and observation, they develop a keen understanding of how to make people trust and admire them.

This ability to charm is particularly effective because most people do not expect manipulation from someone who appears to be so friendly and charismatic. We tend to associate charm with good intentions, assuming that people who are kind, funny, or engaging are also trustworthy. Sociopaths exploit this tendency, using charm as a tool to lower people's defences and gain access to their lives.

In social situations, sociopaths often know how to say the right things to make people feel important or valued. They may compliment others, show interest in their lives, and even offer help or advice. However, these displays of kindness are rarely genuine. Instead, they are part of a calculated effort to ingratiate themselves with others, making it easier to manipulate them later.

It's important to note that not all charming individuals are sociopaths. Many people possess natural charm and use it to build meaningful connections with others. The difference lies in the motivation behind the charm. While most people use charm as a way to connect with others, sociopaths use it as a tool for exploitation.

Superficial Connections

One of the hallmark traits of sociopathy is an inability to form deep emotional connections. While sociopaths may have numerous acquaintances and appear to be well-liked by others, these relationships are almost always superficial. Sociopaths rarely form real emotional bonds because they lack the empathy and emotional depth necessary to connect with others on a meaningful level.

To the outside world, a sociopath may appear to have a large social circle. They may be popular at work, have many friends, or be the life of the party. However, these relationships are built on a foundation of manipulation rather than mutual respect or affection. Sociopaths view relationships as a means to an end—a way to gain something, whether it's power, status, money, or control over others.

In personal relationships, sociopaths often seek out people who can offer them something they want. This could be financial support, social connections, or simply someone to manipulate for their own amusement. Once they have extracted what they need from the relationship, they may discard the other person without hesitation or remorse.

Because sociopaths are unable to form genuine emotional bonds, their relationships tend to be shallow and transactional. They may be able to mimic the behaviours associated with close relationships—spending time with someone, expressing interest in their lives, or offering emotional support—but these actions are driven by self-interest rather than a desire to connect.

Sociopaths are also known for their ability to compartmentalise their lives. They may maintain several different relationships at once, keeping each one separate from the others. This allows them to manipulate multiple people simultaneously without being detected. For example, a sociopath might have a spouse or partner whom they present as their primary relationship, while also engaging in affairs or other manipulative relationships on the side.

Over time, the people in a sociopath's life may begin to notice the lack of emotional depth in their relationship. They may feel that the sociopath is distant or uncaring, even if they initially seemed charming and attentive. This emotional detachment can be confusing and hurtful, especially for those who believed they had formed a close bond with the sociopath.

Faking Emotions

One of the most dangerous tools in a sociopath's arsenal is their ability to fake emotions. While sociopaths lack the capacity for genuine empathy or emotional connection, they are highly skilled at mimicking emotional responses. This allows them to navigate social situations and manipulate others by pretending to feel emotions they do not actually experience.

For example, a sociopath might laugh at a joke they don't find funny, offer sympathy to someone who is upset, or express excitement over an event they don't care about. These emotional displays are typically shallow and calculated, designed to elicit a specific response from others. By mimicking emotions, sociopaths can blend in with those around them and avoid suspicion.

This ability to fake emotions is particularly effective in personal relationships. A sociopath might appear to be a loving partner, offering comfort and support during difficult times. However, these displays of affection are not driven by genuine concern for the other person but by a desire to maintain control over the relationship. The sociopath's goal is to keep their partner emotionally invested in the relationship, making it easier to manipulate them.

Faking emotions also allows sociopaths to avoid accountability for their actions. If a sociopath hurts someone, they may offer a fake apology or express regret, even though they feel no genuine remorse. This can be confusing for the victim, who may be inclined to forgive the sociopath based on their emotional display. In reality, the sociopath is simply using their ability to fake emotions to avoid consequences and maintain control over the situation.

It's important to recognise that while sociopaths can mimic emotions, their emotional displays are often inconsistent or inappropriate for the situation. For example, a sociopath might offer exaggerated sympathy for a minor problem but show little to no reaction in the face of a serious emotional event. This inconsistency can be a red flag for those who are able to see through the sociopath's façade.

Case Study: The Charmer

To illustrate the dangers of sociopathic charm, let's examine a case study of a fictionalised sociopath named Ethan. Ethan is a highly charismatic individual who quickly gains the trust of those around him. He is well-liked at work, has a wide circle of friends, and is known for his charm and wit. However, beneath this charming exterior lies a much darker nature.

Ethan meets Sarah, a successful professional in her mid-thirties, at a social event. He quickly charms her with his intelligence, humour, and apparent interest in her life. He seems to understand her on a deep level, and she is drawn to his magnetic personality. Within a few weeks, they are dating, and Sarah believes she has found her perfect match.

At first, Ethan seems like the ideal partner. He is attentive, affectionate, and supportive. He showers Sarah with compliments, takes her on romantic dates, and makes her feel like the most important person in the world. However, as the relationship progresses, subtle signs of manipulation begin to emerge.

Ethan starts to isolate Sarah from her friends and family, subtly suggesting that they don't have her best interests at heart. He criticises her work, making her doubt her abilities, and convinces her to rely on him for emotional support. At the same time, he begins to take control of her finances, insisting that he can manage them better than she can.

Whenever Sarah expresses concern about the relationship, Ethan fakes emotional responses to manipulate her. He may cry and apologise, claiming that he is trying his best and that he truly loves her. These emotional displays confuse Sarah, making her doubt her instincts and forgive Ethan's behaviour.

Over time, Ethan's true nature becomes more apparent. He is controlling, manipulative, and emotionally abusive. He cares little for Sarah's well-being and is primarily interested in maintaining control over her life. By the time Sarah realises the extent of Ethan's manipulation, she is deeply entangled in the relationship and finds it difficult to leave.

Ethan's story illustrates how sociopaths use charm and emotional manipulation to gain control over their victims. By pretending to be the perfect partner, Ethan is able to deceive Sarah and exploit her for his own gain. This case study serves as a warning to be cautious of those who seem too good to be true, as their charm may be masking a much darker reality.

Manipulating First Impressions

One of the most effective tools in a sociopath's arsenal is their ability to manipulate first impressions. First impressions are powerful because they shape the way people perceive each other in the long term. A positive first impression can make people more likely to trust, admire, and overlook potential red flags.

Sociopaths understand the importance of first impressions and use their charm to make a strong initial impact. Whether it's in a job interview, a first date, or a social gathering, sociopaths know how to present themselves in the most favourable light. They are skilled at reading the social cues of others and adapting their behaviour to match what the situation requires.

In a professional setting, a sociopath might charm their way through an interview by appearing confident, knowledgeable, and personable. They may compliment the interviewer, express enthusiasm for the job, and offer well-rehearsed answers to common interview questions. This charm allows them to secure jobs or promotions, even if they lack the qualifications or experience necessary for the position.

On a first date, a sociopath might charm their potential partner by showing interest in their life, asking thoughtful questions, and sharing engaging stories. They may present themselves as the perfect match, expressing admiration for the same hobbies, values, or interests as their date. This initial charm can be disarming, making it difficult for the other person to recognise the sociopath's true intentions.

First impressions are so powerful because they create a cognitive bias known as the halo effect. When someone makes a positive first impression, people are more likely to view their subsequent behaviour in a favourable light. This bias makes it easier for sociopaths to manipulate others, as their charm in the early stages of a relationship or interaction makes people more likely to overlook any negative traits or behaviours that may emerge later.

The mask of charm is one of the most deceptive and dangerous tools that sociopaths use to manipulate and control others. By cultivating a charming exterior, sociopaths are able to hide their true nature, build superficial relationships, and fake emotions to exploit those around them. Whether in personal relationships, social settings, or professional environments, sociopaths use charm to manipulate first impressions and gain power over others.

In the next chapter, we will explore the warning signs and red flags that can help people identify when they are dealing with a sociopath. By understanding these signs, individuals can protect themselves from falling victim to the charm and manipulation of a sociopath.

Chapter 3:

Red Flags in Relationships

Personal relationships are built on trust, empathy, and mutual respect. When these foundations are eroded, a relationship can become a breeding ground for emotional manipulation and abuse. Sociopaths, with their ability to charm and deceive, often enter relationships with ulterior motives, using a range of tactics to control and exploit their partners. Identifying the red flags of sociopathy early in a relationship is critical to avoid becoming entangled in their web of manipulation. This chapter will delve into the early warning signs of sociopathic behaviour in personal relationships, focusing on their strategies for control, emotional manipulation, and psychological abuse.

Early Signs of Manipulation

At the beginning of a relationship with a sociopath, everything may feel like a whirlwind romance. Sociopaths are masters of first impressions, and they often use love-bombing to win their partners over. Love-bombing is a tactic in which the sociopath showers their new partner with excessive affection, compliments, and attention. In the early stages of the relationship, the sociopath may appear to be the perfect partner— attentive, caring, and deeply interested in their partner's life.

This overwhelming display of affection can make the victim feel special, as though they've found someone who truly understands them. They may receive constant text messages, surprise gifts, or declarations of love early on in the relationship. The sociopath's goal is to create an intense emotional connection quickly, leaving their partner feeling bonded and invested before they have time to recognise any red flags.

However, this intense affection is often a red flag in itself. Love-bombing is not about genuine care or affection; it's about control. By moving quickly and overwhelming their partner with attention, the sociopath seeks to gain emotional leverage, making it harder for the partner to detach or see the relationship clearly. Healthy relationships typically develop gradually, with both partners taking time to get to know each other. In contrast, the sociopath pushes for quick intimacy, blurring the lines between authentic emotional connection and manipulation.

Another early sign of manipulation is the sociopath's desire for exclusivity early in the relationship. They may try to isolate their partner emotionally, subtly discouraging them from spending time with friends or family. They might frame this behaviour as a sign of their devotion, insisting that they want to spend all their time together. But in reality, it's about cutting the partner off from their support network, making them more dependent on the sociopath for emotional validation.

The Gradual Control

Once the sociopath has established trust and emotional closeness, they begin to slowly exert control over their partner. This process can be so gradual that the victim often doesn't realise it's happening until they're deeply entangled in the relationship.

One common tactic sociopaths use is isolation. They may start by subtly undermining their partner's relationships with friends and family. For example, they might claim that a close friend is "jealous" of the relationship or that a family member doesn't have the partner's best interests at heart. Over time, they discourage their partner from maintaining outside relationships, leaving the victim increasingly reliant on the sociopath for emotional support.

Isolation can also occur through more direct means. The sociopath may insist that they and their partner spend all their time together, or they might become upset when their partner makes plans without them. This gradual isolation serves to cut the partner off from their social network, making it easier for the sociopath to exert control without interference from others.

Another hallmark of sociopathic manipulation is gaslighting. Gaslighting is a psychological tactic in which the sociopath causes their partner to doubt their own perceptions, memories, or feelings. The sociopath may lie, deny things they've said or done, or twist events to make their partner feel confused and disoriented. Over time, the victim begins to doubt their own sense of reality, making it easier for the sociopath to control and manipulate them.

For example, the sociopath might deny saying something hurtful, even though their partner clearly remembers the conversation. When the partner questions this, the sociopath might respond with phrases like, "You're being too sensitive," or "You're imagining things." This constant manipulation leads the partner to question their own judgment, making them more dependent on the sociopath for validation and guidance.

Guilt-tripping is another common tactic sociopaths use to control their partners. They may make their partner feel guilty for expressing independence or for wanting to spend time with other people. For example, if the partner wants to go out with friends, the sociopath might say, "I guess you don't care about me as much as I thought," or, "I just want to spend time with you, but if you don't feel the same, I understand." This manipulation is designed to make the partner feel guilty for prioritising their own needs, pushing them to comply with the sociopath's demands.

Over time, these tactics create a dynamic in which the sociopath holds all the power. The partner becomes increasingly isolated, unsure of themselves, and dependent on the sociopath for emotional validation and guidance. This gradual control is often difficult to detect because it happens so slowly and subtly, but it is a key red flag in relationships with sociopaths.

Inconsistent Behaviour

Another hallmark of sociopathic manipulation is inconsistent behaviour. Sociopaths may oscillate between being loving and attentive one moment and cold and distant the next. This inconsistency keeps the partner off-balance, always wondering what they did to cause the change in behaviour. The sociopath's goal is to create a dynamic in which their partner is constantly seeking their approval, desperate to regain the affection that was so freely given in the beginning.

This inconsistent behaviour often manifests as sudden shifts in mood or attention. For example, the sociopath may be highly affectionate and attentive for days or weeks, making their partner feel loved and secure. Then, seemingly out of nowhere, they may withdraw emotionally, becoming distant or even hostile. When the partner tries to address the change in behaviour, the sociopath may respond with irritation or indifference, making the partner feel like they're being overly needy or demanding.

These fluctuations in behaviour create a sense of emotional dependency. The partner becomes fixated on trying to recapture the warmth and affection they received early in the relationship, often blaming themselves for the sociopath's withdrawal. This cycle of affection and rejection creates a powerful bond, as the partner becomes increasingly focused on pleasing the sociopath in the hopes of receiving love and validation in return.

This behaviour is sometimes referred to as the intermittent reinforcement cycle, a concept rooted in psychology. When a person receives inconsistent rewards—sometimes receiving affection and sometimes being ignored—they become more invested in the relationship, as they are always hoping for the next "reward" of affection. Sociopaths exploit this psychological principle to keep their partners emotionally dependent and compliant.

Lack of Empathy

One of the most significant red flags in a relationship with a sociopath is their lack of empathy. While sociopaths can mimic emotional responses and appear to be caring, they are fundamentally unable to understand or feel the emotions of others. This lack of empathy becomes particularly apparent in moments of crisis or vulnerability, when their partner needs genuine emotional support.

For example, if their partner is going through a difficult time—such as the loss of a loved one, a health crisis, or a stressful work situation—the sociopath may appear indifferent or even annoyed by their partner's emotional needs. They may offer superficial sympathy but quickly become frustrated if their partner continues to seek support. Over time, this lack of emotional responsiveness can leave the partner feeling isolated, as they are unable to rely on the sociopath for comfort or understanding.

In some cases, sociopaths may use their partner's vulnerability as an opportunity for manipulation. Instead of offering support, they may exploit their partner's emotional state to gain control. For example, if their partner is going through a difficult time, the sociopath might use guilt or blame to make the partner feel responsible for their own distress. This lack of empathy is a clear red flag that something is wrong in the relationship.

It's important to recognise that while sociopaths can fake emotional responses, their inability to truly connect with their partner on an emotional level will eventually become apparent. In moments when genuine empathy and care are needed, the sociopath's emotional detachment will be unmistakable.

Emotional and Psychological Abuse

Sociopaths are skilled at using emotional and psychological abuse to control their partners. This abuse often takes the form of subtle manipulation tactics that are difficult to recognise at first but become more apparent over time. Some of the most common forms of emotional and psychological abuse used by sociopaths include blaming, guilt-tripping, and gaslighting.

Blaming is a tactic in which the sociopath shifts responsibility for their actions onto their partner. For example, if the sociopath behaves in a hurtful or manipulative way, they may blame their partner for "making" them act that way. They might say things like, "If you hadn't done that, I wouldn't have reacted this way," or, "It's your fault I got angry." By shifting the blame, the sociopath avoids taking responsibility for their behaviour and makes their partner feel guilty for causing conflict.

Guilt-tripping is another common tactic used by sociopaths to control their partners. They may make their partner feel guilty for expressing independence, setting boundaries, or standing up for themselves. For example, if the partner wants to spend time with friends, the sociopath might say, "I thought you cared about me, but I guess I was wrong," or, "I guess you don't love me as much as I thought." This manipulation tactic is designed to make the partner feel guilty for prioritising their own needs, pushing them to comply with the sociopath's demands.

Gaslighting, as discussed earlier, is a psychological tactic in which the sociopath causes their partner to doubt their own perceptions, memories, or feelings. This constant manipulation leads the partner to question their own sense of reality, making them more dependent on the sociopath for validation and guidance.

Together, these tactics create a dynamic in which the sociopath holds all the power in the relationship, leaving their partner feeling confused, disoriented, and emotionally dependent.

Case Example: June and Pete

To illustrate how these red flags manifest in real life, let's consider the case of June and Pete, a fictionalised but representative example of a relationship with a sociopath.

When June first met Pete, he seemed like the perfect partner. He was charming, attentive, and deeply interested in her life. He showered her with compliments and affection, often sending her sweet messages throughout the day. June felt like she had found her soulmate, and the relationship moved quickly. Within weeks, Pete was telling her that he loved her and wanted to spend the rest of his life with her.

However, as the relationship progressed, June began to notice subtle changes in Pete's behaviour. He started to make negative comments about her friends, suggesting that they were jealous of their relationship. He encouraged her to spend less time with them and more time with him. Over time, June found herself becoming more isolated, as she stopped seeing her friends and focused all her attention on Pete.

Pete also began to exhibit inconsistent behaviour. One day, he would be loving and affectionate, making June feel secure in the relationship. The next day, he would withdraw emotionally, becoming distant and cold. When June asked him what was wrong, he would dismiss her concerns, telling her that she was being too sensitive or imagining things.

As the relationship continued, Pete's manipulation became more apparent. He often blamed June for his outbursts, telling her that if she hadn't said or done certain things, he wouldn't have gotten angry. He also used guilt-tripping to make June feel responsible for the problems in their relationship. Whenever June tried to assert her independence or set boundaries, Pete would make her feel guilty, suggesting that she didn't care about him or wasn't committed to the relationship.

Over time, June became emotionally dependent on Pete, constantly seeking his approval and validation. She felt confused and disoriented, unsure of what was real and what wasn't. It wasn't until she confided in a friend and began researching sociopathic behaviour that she realised what was happening.

Conclusion

Recognising the red flags of sociopathic behaviour in personal relationships is crucial for protecting oneself from emotional manipulation and abuse. Early signs of manipulation, such as love-bombing and isolation, can be difficult to detect but are key indicators of a toxic relationship. As the relationship progresses, tactics like gaslighting, guilt-tripping, and emotional inconsistency become more apparent, leaving the victim confused, isolated, and emotionally dependent on the sociopath.

By understanding these red flags, individuals can protect themselves from falling victim to the charm and manipulation of a sociopath. In the next chapter, we will explore how sociopaths operate in professional settings, using similar tactics to manipulate and control their colleagues and superiors.

Chapter 4:

Sociopaths in the Workplace

The workplace is a complex environment where individuals interact, compete, and collaborate to achieve professional goals. For most people, these interactions are guided by ethics, empathy, and a sense of teamwork. However, for a sociopath, the workplace represents a stage for manipulation, control, and self-serving behaviour. Sociopaths in the workplace can wreak havoc on teams, create toxic environments, and advance their own careers at the expense of others. In this chapter, we will explore how sociopaths operate in the workplace, particularly in corporate settings, and provide practical guidance for recognising and dealing with them.

The Corporate Sociopath

Sociopaths thrive in environments that reward power, control, and status, making the corporate world an ideal playing field for their manipulative tendencies. In many cases, corporate sociopaths are highly skilled at masking their true nature, presenting themselves as charming, competent, and team-oriented individuals while hiding their self-serving motives beneath a façade of professionalism.

The corporate sociopath excels in environments where competition is fierce and interpersonal relationships are critical to success. They leverage their lack of empathy, using colleagues as stepping stones on their path to power. These individuals may initially come across as charismatic and dedicated, earning the trust and admiration of their peers and superiors. But beneath this polished exterior lies a ruthless drive to succeed, often at the expense of others.

One key characteristic of the corporate sociopath is their ability to manipulate office dynamics to their advantage. They are experts at understanding what makes people tick and use this knowledge to position themselves favourably. For example, they might play the role of the "go-getter" who is always willing to take on extra work, or they may cultivate relationships with higher-ups to secure promotions or favourable treatment. These actions are not motivated by a genuine desire to contribute to the team or the company, but rather by a cold, calculated drive to further their own interests.

Another tactic employed by corporate sociopaths is sabotaging colleagues while maintaining the appearance of a team player. They may undermine a coworker's work, spread rumours, or subtly diminish someone else's accomplishments while positioning themselves as the superior candidate for a promotion or leadership role. By manipulating the perceptions of those around them, sociopaths can create divisions within the team, making it easier for them to advance while others struggle.

In the corporate world, where ambition and success are often valued above all else, sociopaths can blend in easily. Their ability to charm and manipulate makes it difficult for others to see through their façade until significant damage has been done. Recognising the signs of a corporate sociopath early on can help protect yourself and your colleagues from falling victim to their schemes.

Using Power to Manipulate

When a sociopath ascends to a leadership position, the stakes become even higher. With the added power and authority that comes with managerial roles, sociopaths are in a prime position to exploit others for personal gain. The sociopath in power is often characterised by a complete disregard for the well-being of their employees and a willingness to manipulate situations to their advantage.

One of the most common ways that sociopathic leaders manipulate their subordinates is by taking credit for others' work. In this scenario, the sociopath ensures that their employees are putting in the effort and producing results, but when it comes time to report progress to higher-ups, the sociopath steps in and claims the achievements as their own. This not only undermines the efforts of hardworking employees but also positions the sociopath as an indispensable leader in the eyes of upper management.

At the same time, sociopaths in leadership positions often shift blame onto their subordinates when things go wrong. If a project fails or targets are not met, the sociopathic leader will deflect responsibility and point fingers at their team, protecting their own reputation while throwing their employees under the bus. This tactic creates a culture of fear and mistrust, where employees are constantly worried about being scapegoated for issues beyond their control.

Sociopathic leaders are also notorious for setting unrealistic expectations for their employees. They may assign impossible workloads, demand unreasonable hours, or expect perfection in every task, all while offering little to no support. When employees inevitably struggle to meet these demands, the sociopath uses this as an opportunity to criticise and belittle them, reinforcing their control and dominance.

Perhaps the most insidious aspect of a sociopathic leader's behaviour is their ability to manipulate higher-ups for personal advancement. Sociopaths in leadership positions are often highly skilled at managing their relationships with those above them, ensuring that their bosses see them in a positive light. They may go out of their way to appear competent, charming, and indispensable to the company's success, all while creating chaos and dysfunction within their own teams. This manipulation allows them to continue advancing within the organisation, even as their subordinates suffer under their toxic leadership.

Office Politics and Sabotage

In addition to directly manipulating employees and higher-ups, sociopaths in the workplace are experts at navigating the complex world of office politics. They thrive in environments where gossip, alliances, and backstabbing are common, and they use these dynamics to their advantage.

One of the most common tactics employed by workplace sociopaths is pitting people against each other. They may engage in office gossip, subtly spreading rumours or planting seeds of doubt about colleagues. By doing so, they create divisions within the team, causing coworkers to mistrust one another and focus on internal conflicts rather than their work. Meanwhile, the sociopath positions themselves as the one person who can be trusted, gaining influence over those who have been isolated by their tactics.

Sociopaths also excel at controlling narratives within the workplace. They are masters at framing situations in a way that benefits them while making others look bad. For example, if a project is going well, the sociopath will ensure that they are seen as the driving force behind its success. If a project is struggling, they will subtly suggest that it is someone else's fault, even if they were directly responsible for the failure. This manipulation of narratives allows the sociopath to maintain a positive image, even when their actions have been detrimental to the team or company.

In more extreme cases, sociopaths may engage in direct sabotage of their colleagues. This could involve withholding important information, deliberately making mistakes to cause others to fail, or even spreading lies about a colleague's performance or behaviour. The goal of this sabotage is to eliminate competition and ensure that the sociopath remains in a position of power and influence within the company.

Office politics can be a challenging environment for anyone to navigate, but when a sociopath is involved, the stakes become even higher. Their ability to manipulate relationships, control narratives, and create divisions can have a devastating impact on team dynamics and overall workplace morale.

Recognising the Sociopathic Boss

While sociopaths in leadership positions can be difficult to identify due to their charm and manipulative skills, there are several key traits that can help you recognise a sociopathic boss. Understanding these traits is crucial for protecting yourself and your career from their toxic influence.

1. Lack of Concern for Employee Well-Being: Sociopathic bosses have little to no regard for the well-being of their employees. They may expect their staff to work long hours without adequate compensation, fail to provide support or resources, and show no empathy for personal or professional struggles. Their focus is solely on their own success, and they view their employees as tools to be used rather than individuals with needs and feelings.

2. Micromanagement: Sociopathic leaders often exert control over every aspect of their employees' work, constantly monitoring their performance and dictating how tasks should be completed. This micromanagement is a way for the sociopath to maintain dominance over their subordinates, ensuring that they are always in control and that no one can operate independently.

3. Shifting Blame: As mentioned earlier, one of the hallmark traits of a sociopathic boss is their tendency to shift blame onto their employees when things go wrong. They will never take responsibility for mistakes or failures, instead pointing fingers at those below them. This creates a toxic work environment where employees

live in fear of being scapegoated for issues beyond their control.

4. Manipulating Higher-Ups for Personal Advancement: Sociopathic bosses are highly skilled at managing their relationships with higher-ups, ensuring that they are seen in a positive light by those in positions of power. They may charm their superiors, present themselves as indispensable to the company, and downplay any issues within their team. This manipulation allows them to continue advancing within the organisation, even as their leadership creates dysfunction and chaos.

Recognising these traits in a boss is the first step toward protecting yourself from their toxic influence. If you suspect that your boss may be a sociopath, it's important to take steps to safeguard your well-being and professional reputation.

Real-World Scenario: The Sociopathic Manager

To illustrate the impact of a sociopathic leader on a workplace, let's consider the fictional case of Michael, a manager at a mid-sized tech company.

When Michael first joined the company, he quickly made a positive impression on both his team and upper management. He was charismatic, confident, and appeared to be deeply invested in the success of the company. His superiors saw him as a rising star, and within a year, he was promoted to a managerial position.

However, once Michael assumed his leadership role, things began to change. He became increasingly controlling, micromanaging his team's every move and setting unrealistic expectations for their performance. He demanded long hours, often expecting his employees to stay late into the night without offering any additional compensation or time off. When projects went well,

Michael took full credit, presenting the results as his own accomplishments to upper management.

When projects went well, Michael took full credit, presenting the results as his own accomplishments to upper management. But when things went wrong, he deftly shifted blame to his team. If a project failed to meet a deadline or did not achieve expected results, Michael would call an emergency meeting, often singling out team members and publicly questioning their competence. "If you had just followed my directions," he would say, "we wouldn't be in this situation." This behaviour instilled fear among his team members, leading them to feel insecure and unsure of their abilities.

Michael's approach to management created a culture of anxiety and mistrust. Team members began to isolate themselves from one another, worried about being blamed for failures or criticised for their performance. They were reluctant to collaborate, fearing that any idea they presented could be co-opted by Michael for his gain. The once vibrant and creative atmosphere of the team dwindled, replaced by a suffocating environment where employees were more concerned about self-preservation than collaboration.

Sabotage and Gossip

Behind the scenes, Michael's sociopathic tendencies manifested through office politics and manipulation. He would often engage in office gossip, spreading rumours about team members to pit them against each other. For instance, he would casually mention to one employee that another had doubts about their work ethic or that they were seeking a promotion. This sowed discord among team members, causing rivalries and divisions that further served his agenda.

Michael also subtly undermined his team's efforts. If someone proposed an innovative idea, he would agree to it in front of the group but later quietly tell upper management that he was sceptical about its viability. When the idea failed, he would be quick to remind the team that it was theirs, not his. This form of sabotage was a calculated tactic to ensure that he remained in control while diminishing the confidence of his team.

Recognising the Signs

As the months passed, employees began to recognise the red flags of Michael's sociopathic behaviour. They noticed his inconsistent emotional engagement; one moment he would be effusive in praise, and the next, he would be cold and dismissive. This emotional rollercoaster kept the team on edge, desperate for his approval and fearful of his wrath.

The team members also began to share their experiences with one another, realising they were not alone in feeling manipulated and controlled. They recognised the importance of documenting Michael's behaviour, keeping records of conversations, decisions made in meetings, and instances where he shifted blame. This documentation became crucial for protecting their professional reputations and ensuring that they had evidence of his manipulative tactics should they ever need to escalate their concerns to HR or upper management.

How to Deal with a Sociopath at Work

Navigating a workplace with a sociopathic manager can be incredibly challenging, but there are strategies employees can employ to protect themselves and mitigate the impact of their sociopathic boss:

1. Set Boundaries: It's essential to establish clear boundaries with a sociopathic boss. This includes limiting the time you spend alone with them and being cautious about sharing personal information. Sociopaths often use intimate details against their victims, so maintaining a professional distance can help protect you.

2. Document Everything: Keep meticulous records of your work, conversations, and interactions with the sociopath. Document instances where they shift blame, take credit for your work, or engage in manipulative

behaviour. This documentation can serve as crucial evidence if you need to report their behaviour to HR or seek a transfer.

3. Seek Support: Reach out to colleagues who may also be affected by the sociopath's behaviour. Forming alliances with coworkers can provide emotional support and reinforce your collective experiences. Discussing your concerns with trusted colleagues can help you gain perspective and validate your feelings.

4. Focus on Your Work: While it can be tempting to engage in the office politics that sociopaths thrive on, focus on your work and maintain a high standard of performance. By excelling in your role, you create a buffer against the sociopath's manipulations, making it harder for them to undermine your contributions.

5. Consider Escalation: If the situation becomes intolerable, consider discussing your concerns with HR or upper management. Present your documentation as evidence of the sociopath's behaviour and the impact it

has had on you and your colleagues. While this can be a daunting step, it may be necessary for your well-being and that of your coworkers.

6. Plan Your Exit: If the sociopath's behaviour does not improve and continues to create a toxic work environment, it may be time to consider seeking employment elsewhere. Prioritising your mental health and well-being is crucial, and sometimes the best option is to remove yourself from the toxic situation entirely.

Conclusion

Sociopaths in the workplace can create toxic environments that undermine teamwork, morale, and productivity. They excel in competitive corporate settings, using their charm and manipulative skills to climb the ladder while sabotaging their colleagues. Recognising the signs of a sociopathic boss—such as a lack of concern for employee well-being, micromanagement, blame-shifting, and manipulative behaviour—can empower individuals to protect themselves.

By understanding how sociopaths operate in the workplace and employing strategies to mitigate their impact, employees can navigate the complexities of corporate life with greater awareness and resilience. The next chapter will explore how sociopaths manipulate relationships in social settings, shedding light on their tactics and providing insights for protecting oneself outside of work.

Chapter 5:

Techniques Sociopaths Use to Stay Hidden

Sociopaths are masters of disguise, often operating under the radar of detection, blending into their surroundings while subtly manipulating those around them. Unlike the violent, erratic sociopaths depicted in popular media, functioning sociopaths are far more insidious, using psychological tactics to remain hidden in plain sight. By employing methods such as gaslighting, pathological lying, and masking emotions, they manipulate others into questioning their own perceptions while gaining sympathy and deflecting blame. In this chapter, we will delve into these techniques, revealing how sociopaths manage to evade suspicion and maintain control over their victims.

Gaslighting and Psychological Manipulation

One of the most powerful tools in a sociopath's arsenal is gaslighting, a form of psychological manipulation designed to make the victim doubt their own memory, perception, and even sanity. The term originates from the 1944 film Gaslight, in which a husband manipulates his wife into believing she is losing her mind by subtly altering their environment and denying the changes when she notices them. Similarly, sociopaths use gaslighting to destabilise their victims' sense of reality.

Gaslighting begins subtly, often in the form of small lies or denials. A sociopath may claim they never said something they did, or they might dismiss their victim's feelings as irrational. Over time, these small distortions build up, causing the victim to question their memory and judgment. The goal is to create a state of confusion, where the victim becomes increasingly dependent on the sociopath for validation and interpretation of reality.

Common Gaslighting Tactics

1. Denial of Reality: Sociopaths will flat-out deny things that have happened, making their victim question what they know to be true. For instance, if the sociopath insults someone and later the victim confronts them about it, they may respond, "I never said that," or "You're making things up."

2. Twisting Facts: They are skilled at distorting the truth. If confronted with evidence of their misbehaviour, sociopaths might turn the situation around, suggesting the victim is overly sensitive or misunderstood their intentions. Statements like, "You're just being dramatic" or "You always overreact" are typical ways they twist the narrative to place the blame on the victim.

3. Undermining Confidence: Gaslighting often involves undermining the victim's confidence in their own decision-making abilities. The sociopath might belittle their opinions or mock their concerns, saying things like, "You're too emotional to make rational decisions," leading the victim to doubt their own judgment.

4. Creating Chaos: Sociopaths thrive in environments where others are confused or uncertain. They may intentionally create situations of uncertainty or ambiguity to keep their victims off-balance. By shifting blame or giving conflicting information, they create a web of confusion in which the victim cannot discern the truth from manipulation.

Over time, gaslighting causes the victim to feel isolated, anxious, and uncertain of their own reality. The sociopath becomes the person the victim relies on to "explain" what is real and what is not, giving the sociopath immense power and control.

Playing the Victim

Sociopaths are experts at manipulating people's emotions, and one of their most effective techniques is playing the victim. By casting themselves as the wronged party, sociopaths gain sympathy and deflect responsibility for their actions. This tactic not only disarms their victims but also serves to shift blame onto others, making it difficult to hold them accountable for their behaviour.

How Sociopaths Use Victimhood to Manipulate

1. Reversing Blame: When confronted with their misdeeds, sociopaths often turn the tables, claiming that they are the ones who have been mistreated. For

example, if they are accused of lying, they might respond with, "I can't believe you think that of me. After everything I've done for you, this is how you treat me?" This tactic causes the victim to feel guilty for confronting them and shifts the focus away from the sociopath's behaviour.

2. Exploiting Sympathy: Sociopaths excel at eliciting sympathy from others by portraying themselves as helpless or oppressed. They may fabricate stories of past abuse, trauma, or mistreatment to gain the trust and pity of their victims. People naturally want to help those who seem vulnerable, and sociopaths exploit this instinct to their advantage.

3. Creating Drama: Playing the victim often involves creating dramatic, emotionally charged situations where the sociopath can garner attention and sympathy. They may stage conflicts or crises that cast them in a sympathetic light, positioning themselves as misunderstood or unfairly targeted by others.

The goal of playing the victim is to create a dynamic in which the sociopath is seen as someone who deserves protection and care. This not only deflects attention from their manipulative behaviour but also makes it harder for their victims to hold them accountable without feeling guilty.

Pathological Lying

Lying is second nature to sociopaths. They engage in pathological lying, effortlessly weaving complex webs of deception without any apparent guilt or remorse. What sets sociopaths apart from ordinary liars is their ability to lie convincingly and often without any obvious motivation. They may lie about trivial matters just as easily as they do about significant ones, leaving their victims unsure of what to believe.

Why Sociopaths Lie

1. Control: Lying allows sociopaths to control the narrative and manipulate how others perceive them. By

fabricating stories, they can present themselves in whatever light serves their interests, whether that's as a hero, victim, or expert.

2. Avoiding Responsibility: Lies are a way for sociopaths to evade accountability for their actions. If they are caught in wrongdoing, they simply lie to cover it up, often with such confidence and consistency that others begin to doubt their own perceptions.

3. Testing Boundaries: Sociopaths sometimes lie simply to see how far they can push people's trust. They enjoy the thrill of manipulating others and watching as their lies go unquestioned. This helps them gauge how much control they have over their victims.

4. Creating Confusion: Lying is also a tool to create confusion and chaos. By giving conflicting stories or contradicting themselves, sociopaths muddy the waters, making it difficult for their victims to discern the truth.

Pathological lying can be difficult to detect because sociopaths are highly skilled at maintaining consistency in their lies, often mixing them with elements of truth to make them more believable. Over time, these lies compound, creating a distorted reality that the sociopath controls.

Masking Emotions

Sociopaths are often described as lacking empathy, but they are adept at mimicking emotions to appear normal and manipulate others. While they may not actually feel empathy, concern, or love, they can convincingly perform these emotions when it serves their interests.

How Sociopaths Mask Their Emotions

1. Mimicking Empathy: Sociopaths observe how others respond in emotional situations and learn to replicate these responses. For example, if someone is grieving, the sociopath might offer condolences or comforting words, but these gestures are superficial, meant to create the

appearance of empathy rather than stemming from genuine concern.

2. Faking Concern: Sociopaths may show false concern for others, particularly when it allows them to maintain control or gain favour. For instance, they might act worried about a friend's well-being, not because they care, but because it gives them an opportunity to exert influence or gather information.

3. Projecting a "Perfect" Image: Many sociopaths go to great lengths to present themselves as kind, generous, or trustworthy. They are keenly aware of how they are perceived and will adjust their behaviour to fit the expectations of those around them. This can make it difficult for their victims to see their true nature.

While sociopaths can convincingly mask their emotions in the short term, over time, their lack of genuine emotional depth becomes apparent. Their responses to emotionally charged situations often feel hollow or scripted, and they may struggle to maintain consistent displays of emotion over extended periods.

Subtle Forms of Abuse

While sociopaths are capable of overt manipulation and control, much of their abuse is subtle and insidious, leaving victims feeling confused and questioning themselves. Unlike physical or overt emotional abuse, which can be more easily recognised, sociopathic abuse often takes the form of emotional manipulation, gaslighting, and psychological control.

Subtle Abusive Tactics

1. Silent Treatment: Sociopaths may use the silent treatment as a way to punish or control their victims. By withholding communication and affection, they create an atmosphere of uncertainty and insecurity, leaving the victim desperate for their approval.

2. Love-Bombing and Withdrawal: Early in a relationship, sociopaths may engage in love-bombing, showering their victim with affection, attention, and compliments. However, once they have gained the victim's trust, they may suddenly withdraw, leaving the victim confused and anxious to regain their affection.

3. Triangulation: Sociopaths often use triangulation to create competition and jealousy among their victims. They may compare their victim to someone else, making the victim feel inadequate or insecure. This tactic keeps the victim on edge, constantly seeking the sociopath's approval.

These subtle forms of abuse are difficult to recognise because they often seem benign on the surface. However, over time, they erode the victim's sense of self-worth and create a cycle of dependency on the sociopath.

Case Example: The Sociopath in the Family

Consider the story of a sociopath who gradually gains control over a family member, using a combination of gaslighting, playing the victim, and emotional manipulation. Megan, a successful professional in her early 30s, begins to notice changes in her brother, Daniel, after he moves back in with their parents following a failed business venture.

At first, Daniel is charming and seemingly grateful for the support of his family. He spends time with them, offering to help around the house and making an effort to reconnect with Megan. However, over time, Megan starts to notice small inconsistencies in his stories. When confronted, Daniel denies any wrongdoing, claiming Megan is imagining things. "I think you're just stressed from work," he says, brushing off her concerns.

As the months go by, Daniel begins to take advantage of their parents' generosity, asking for money and making excuses for not finding a new job. When Megan tries to intervene, Daniel plays the victim, telling their parents that Megan is being unfair and unsupportive. He insists he is doing his best but that life has been hard on him, eliciting sympathy from their parents and causing tension between Megan and the rest of the family.

Megan becomes increasingly isolated, doubting her own perceptions and feeling guilty for questioning Daniel. It isn't until she seeks advice from a therapist that she begins to see the patterns of gaslighting, manipulation, and control that Daniel has employed to keep the family in his grip.

This chapter has explored the sophisticated techniques sociopaths use to remain hidden, manipulating those around them with gaslighting, playing the victim, pathological lying, and masking their emotions. These tactics, while subtle, can have devastating effects on their victims, leaving them confused, isolated, and unsure of reality. Recognising these red flags is the first step in breaking free from a sociopath's control.

Chapter 6: Identifying Sociopathic Behaviour in Daily Life

Sociopathy, or antisocial personality disorder (ASPD), is often associated with extreme or overtly violent behaviours. However, in daily life, many sociopaths go unnoticed due to their ability to blend in and manipulate their surroundings with subtle, calculated actions. Recognising sociopathic behaviour requires an awareness of the small, often overlooked signs that can indicate a deeper pattern of manipulation and deceit. This chapter aims to help readers understand the subtle signs of sociopathy, detect inconsistencies in behaviour, and trust their instincts when something feels off in a relationship or interaction.

Subtle Signs of Sociopathy

While media portrayals of sociopaths tend to focus on extreme examples—violent criminals or power-hungry manipulators—most sociopaths operate more subtly in everyday life. They may not stand out as dangerous or malicious but can nonetheless inflict significant harm on those around them through emotional manipulation, deceit, and exploitation.

Excessive Flattery

One of the most common early signs of sociopathy is excessive flattery. Sociopaths are skilled at reading people and understanding what they want to hear. They may use flattery to disarm their target and gain their trust. This flattery often feels over-the-top or insincere, but it can be difficult to resist, especially when it is accompanied by other forms of charm and attention.

For example, in the early stages of a relationship—whether romantic, social, or professional—a sociopath may shower their target with compliments. They may praise everything from their intelligence and appearance to their work ethic and personality. This can feel flattering at first, but over time, it may become apparent that the sociopath is using these compliments to manipulate their target's emotions and gain influence over them.

Key indicators of excessive flattery include:

- Compliments that feel disproportionate or exaggerated.

- Flattery that seems to be used strategically to gain favour or trust.

- A sense of discomfort or suspicion that the flattery is not genuine.

Manipulating Small Situations

Sociopaths often begin their manipulation with small, seemingly inconsequential situations. They may test boundaries by lying about trivial matters or manipulating events to see how others react. These small acts of deceit or manipulation serve as practice for larger, more significant manipulations later on.

For instance, a sociopath might lie about something insignificant, like why they were late to an appointment or whether they completed a task at work. If the lie goes unnoticed or unchallenged, they feel emboldened to continue lying and manipulating in more significant ways. Over time, these small lies and manipulations can add up, creating a pattern of deceit that is difficult to unravel.

Signs of small-scale manipulation include:

- Stories that don't quite add up but seem too trivial to confront.

- A tendency to twist the truth or avoid taking responsibility for minor mistakes.

- Frequent use of excuses or explanations that deflect blame.

Being Overly Competitive

Sociopaths often have a strong need to win or be seen as superior to others. This can manifest as excessive competitiveness in both professional and personal situations. While competition is normal in certain contexts, sociopaths take it to an extreme, viewing every interaction as a contest they must win—whether it's a debate, a project at work, or even a simple conversation.

In a professional setting, this might look like a colleague who constantly undermines others, takes credit for work they didn't do, or manipulates office dynamics to position themselves as the star performer. In personal relationships, it may involve turning every discussion into a competition, belittling others' achievements, or creating rivalries between friends or family members.

Key signs of excessive competitiveness:

- A constant need to one-up others or prove superiority.

- A willingness to bend the rules or sabotage others to win.

- Difficulty accepting others' success without resentment or jealousy.

Inconsistent Stories and Lies

Sociopaths are skilled liars, but their lies can be inconsistent over time. They may tell different versions of the same story to different people, or they may change their story when confronted with evidence that contradicts their previous statements. While they are often adept at deflecting blame and explaining away these inconsistencies, recognising these patterns of deceit is crucial in identifying sociopathic behaviour.

Recognising Patterns of Deception

One way to identify sociopaths is to pay attention to inconsistent stories. For example, a sociopath might tell one person that they were out of town for the weekend, but later tell another person they were at home working. When confronted about the inconsistency, they may deny ever saying the first story or claim the other person misunderstood.

Sociopaths often use lies to manipulate situations to their advantage, whether it's gaining sympathy, avoiding responsibility, or controlling the narrative. While individual lies may seem harmless, over time, these inconsistencies can reveal a pattern of deceit and manipulation.

How to spot inconsistencies:

- Pay attention to details that change between different versions of the same story.

- Look for contradictions between what the person says and what they do.

- Notice if the person becomes defensive or evasive when questioned about their stories.

Trusting Your Instincts

One of the most powerful tools in identifying sociopathic behaviour is trusting your instincts. Sociopaths are skilled at creating confusion and doubt, often making their victims second-guess themselves. However, most people have an innate sense when something feels off in a relationship or interaction. Ignoring these gut feelings can lead to prolonged exposure to manipulation and harm.

The Importance of Listening to Your Gut

When interacting with a sociopath, you may experience a vague sense of discomfort or unease, even if you can't pinpoint why. You might feel like the person is too good to be true, or that their stories don't quite add up. These feelings are your instincts trying to warn you that something is wrong. Sociopaths often rely on their victims ignoring these early warning signs, allowing the manipulation to continue unchecked.

How to trust your instincts:

- Pay attention to any sense of discomfort, even if you can't immediately identify its cause.

- Don't dismiss your feelings or rationalise away red flags.

- Take note of any patterns of behaviour that make you feel uneasy or confused.

Trusting your instincts doesn't mean jumping to conclusions or accusing someone of being a sociopath based on a single interaction. Instead, it's about being aware of your feelings and using them as a guide to further investigate whether someone's behaviour aligns with the patterns discussed in this book.

Practical Tips for Recognition

Identifying sociopathic behaviour in daily life requires a combination of awareness, observation, and intuition. Below are some practical tips to help you recognise manipulative behaviours early in relationships—whether romantic, social, or professional.

1. Take Your Time

Sociopaths often try to rush relationships, whether personal or professional. They may push for a commitment early on, seeking to establish trust and control before the other person has had a chance to fully assess their behaviour. Taking your time in getting to know someone can help you spot red flags before you become too emotionally invested.

- Don't feel pressured to move too quickly in a relationship.

- Pay attention to any attempts to rush decisions or commitments.

- Give yourself time to observe the person's behaviour in different contexts.

2. Watch for Inconsistent Behaviour

Sociopaths often display inconsistent behaviour that doesn't align with their words. For example, they may claim to care about someone's feelings but then act in ways that are hurtful or dismissive. Paying attention to discrepancies between what they say and what they do can help you spot manipulative tendencies.

- Look for contradictions between their words and actions.

- Notice if their behaviour changes depending on who they're interacting with.

- Be cautious if they seem to wear different "masks" in different situations.

3. Set Boundaries Early

Sociopaths often test boundaries to see how much control they can exert over someone. Setting clear boundaries early in a relationship can help you gauge how the person responds to limits. A healthy individual will respect your boundaries, while a sociopath may try to push or manipulate them.

- Be clear about your boundaries and expectations from the beginning.

- Pay attention to how the person responds when you set limits.

- Don't be afraid to enforce your boundaries if they are challenged.

4. Document Suspicious Behaviour

If you suspect that someone may be manipulating or deceiving you, it can be helpful to keep a record of their behaviour. This can include writing down inconsistencies in their stories, noting any manipulative tactics they use, and tracking patterns of behaviour over time. Having a written record can help you identify patterns that may not be obvious at the moment.

- Keep notes of any suspicious or manipulative behaviour.

- Document specific incidents where the person's actions don't align with their words.

- Review your notes over time to see if any patterns emerge.

Interactive Section: Spotting Sociopathic Behaviour

To help readers practice identifying sociopathic behaviour, this interactive section provides scenarios where subtle manipulation tactics are at play. After each scenario, reflect on the behaviour exhibited and consider how you would interpret the interaction.

Scenario 1: The Perfect Partner

You've been dating someone for a few weeks, and they seem too good to be true. They constantly compliment you, agree with everything you say, and are always available to spend time with you. However, they seem to avoid talking about their own past or personal details, often changing the subject when asked.

How would you interpret this behaviour?

- Does the excessive flattery feel genuine, or could it be a tactic to gain your trust quickly?

- Why might they avoid sharing personal details about themselves?

Scenario 2: The Competitive Colleague

At work, you have a colleague who is always the first to volunteer for projects and frequently takes credit for team efforts. When you point out that the success was a group effort, they dismiss your contribution and claim they did the majority of the work.

What red flags do you notice in this interaction?

- Is this person trying to manipulate the situation to appear more competent than they are?

- How might their competitiveness be affecting the team dynamic?

Scenario 3: The Confusing Friend

You have a friend who is always there when you need them, offering advice and support. However, you've noticed that they often tell different versions of the same story to different people. When you ask them about the discrepancies, they become defensive and accuse you of not trusting them.

What manipulation tactics are at play?

- Is this person using deceit to control the narrative and maintain their image?

- How does their defensiveness when questioned reveal their manipulative tendencies?

By practicing these scenarios, you can sharpen your ability to recognise sociopathic behaviour in your own life. Spotting these red flags early can help you protect yourself from manipulation and emotional harm.

This chapter has provided an in-depth exploration of how sociopathic behaviour can manifest in everyday interactions. While sociopaths often use subtle tactics to manipulate and deceive those around them, understanding the signs—such as excessive flattery, inconsistent stories, and manipulative competitiveness—can help you protect yourself from their influence. Remember to trust your instincts, set boundaries, and be vigilant in recognising patterns of deceit and manipulation in your relationships.

Chapter 7:

The Impact of Sociopaths on Victims

The emotional, psychological, and even physical damage inflicted by sociopaths on their victims is profound and far-reaching. Victims often find themselves trapped in cycles of manipulation and abuse, leaving them emotionally drained, self-doubting, and, in many cases, traumatised. This chapter aims to explore the deep impact that sociopaths have on their victims, explaining the various tactics they use, the emotional toll of their abuse, and the journey toward healing and recovery.

Emotional Abuse and Its Effects

Emotional abuse at the hands of a sociopath can be devastating. Unlike physical abuse, emotional abuse is often subtle and difficult to recognise at first. Sociopaths use a range of psychological tactics to undermine their victims' sense of self-worth, making them feel confused, powerless, and ultimately dependent on their abuser.

Victims of sociopathic abuse often experience self-doubt, as sociopaths are skilled at making their victims question their perceptions, feelings, and even their sanity. Through gaslighting, manipulation, and deceit, sociopaths erode their victims' confidence, leaving them unable to trust their own judgment. Over time, this leads to a deep sense of anxiety as the victim becomes hyper vigilant, constantly second-guessing themselves and trying to anticipate the abuser's next move.

In many cases, this prolonged emotional abuse leads to depression. Victims may feel trapped, isolated, and helpless, unsure of how to escape the toxic relationship. They often experience low self-esteem, feeling unworthy of love or respect, and may even blame themselves for the abuse they are enduring. The combination of emotional exhaustion and self-blame creates a perfect storm for trauma, as victims struggle to process their experiences and cope with the overwhelming sense of betrayal and hurt.

The long-term psychological effects of emotional abuse can be severe, including:

- Chronic anxiety and hypervigilance, as victims constantly worry about pleasing the abuser or avoiding conflict.

- Depression, stemming from feelings of helplessness and worthlessness.

- Trust issues, not just with the abuser, but with others in future relationships.

- Emotional numbness or detachment, as a coping mechanism to deal with the constant manipulation and abuse.

- Post-Traumatic Stress Disorder (PTSD) or Complex PTSD, particularly in cases where the emotional abuse has been prolonged and severe.

These psychological wounds can persist long after the relationship with the sociopath has ended, leaving victims to grapple with the aftermath of the abuse.

The Cycle of Manipulation

Sociopaths are masters of manipulation, and they use a variety of tactics to control their victims. One of the most insidious aspects of sociopathic abuse is the cycle of manipulation that keeps victims trapped in the relationship. This cycle often follows a predictable pattern, alternating between periods of intense charm and affection and episodes of emotional abuse and cruelty.

In the beginning of the relationship, the sociopath may engage in love-bombing, showering the victim with attention, compliments, and affection. This creates a sense of euphoria and makes the victim feel special, chosen, and deeply connected to the sociopath. However, once the victim is emotionally invested, the sociopath begins to reveal their true nature, subtly testing the victim's boundaries and introducing small acts of manipulation.

Over time, the sociopath's behaviour becomes increasingly controlling. They may exploit their victim's vulnerabilities—such as insecurities, fears, or past trauma—to make the victim feel dependent on them. The sociopath may isolate the victim from friends and family, making them feel like the sociopath is the only person they can rely on. This creates a toxic dependency, where the victim feels trapped and unable to leave the relationship.

The cycle continues with periods of emotional abuse, where the sociopath may criticise, belittle, or manipulate the victim into feeling unworthy or inadequate. This is often followed by periods of reconciliation, where the sociopath returns to their charming and affectionate behaviour, offering apologies, gifts, or promises of change. This intermittent reinforcement keeps the victim hopeful that the relationship will improve, even though the cycle of abuse inevitably repeats.

The emotional exhaustion caused by this cycle can be overwhelming. Victims may feel like they are constantly walking on eggshells, trying to avoid triggering the sociopath's anger or manipulation. Over time, the victim's sense of self-worth is eroded, and they may come to believe that they deserve the abuse or that they are incapable of escaping the relationship.

Trauma Bonding

One of the most perplexing aspects of sociopathic abuse is the phenomenon of trauma bonding. This occurs when the victim becomes emotionally attached to their abuser, despite the pain and suffering they are enduring. Trauma bonding is a result of the cycle of abuse, where periods of affection and reward are interspersed with episodes of cruelty and punishment.

In a healthy relationship, emotional attachment is based on trust, respect, and mutual care. However, in an abusive relationship with a sociopath, the emotional attachment is based on fear, confusion, and a distorted sense of loyalty. The sociopath uses reward and punishment to create an emotional dependency, making the victim feel grateful for even the smallest acts of kindness or affection.

For example, after a particularly cruel episode of emotional abuse, the sociopath may suddenly become loving and affectionate, apologising for their behaviour and promising to change. The victim, who has been starved of affection and validation, may cling to this moment of tenderness, hoping that the abuser's behaviour will improve. This creates a powerful emotional bond, where the victim becomes increasingly reliant on the abuser for emotional support, even though the support is inconsistent and manipulative.

Trauma bonding can be incredibly difficult to break, as the victim's emotions are tied to the abuser in complex and unhealthy ways. The constant cycle of reward and punishment creates a sense of emotional confusion, where the victim is unable to separate their feelings of love and loyalty from the reality of the abuse they are enduring. This emotional attachment makes it difficult for the victim to leave the relationship, even when they recognise that it is harmful.

Healing and Moving On

Recovering from a relationship with a sociopath is a long and difficult process. However, with time, support, and self-care, it is possible for victims to heal and rebuild their lives. The first step in the healing process is recognising the abuse and acknowledging the reality of what happened. This can be one of the most challenging steps, as victims often blame themselves or struggle to accept that they were manipulated and abused.

Once the victim has recognised the abuse, the next step is to seek help and support. Therapy can be incredibly beneficial for victims of sociopathic abuse, helping them process their emotions, rebuild their self-esteem, and develop healthy coping mechanisms. In particular, therapy can help victims address the trauma they experienced and work through the complex emotions associated with the abuse, including anger, guilt, shame, and sadness.

For many victims, regaining self-esteem is one of the most important aspects of the healing process. Sociopaths often leave their victims feeling worthless and unworthy of love, so rebuilding a sense of self-worth is crucial for moving forward. This may involve setting boundaries, learning to trust oneself again, and rediscovering one's passions and interests outside the toxic relationship.

Practical steps for healing from sociopathic abuse include:

- Therapy: Working with a therapist who specialises in trauma and emotional abuse can help victims process their experiences and develop strategies for healing.

- Building a support network: Reconnecting with friends, family, or support groups can provide emotional support and validation during the recovery process.

- Self-care: Taking time for self-care—whether through exercise, hobbies, meditation, or journaling—can help victims reconnect with themselves and prioritise their well-being.

- Setting boundaries: Learning to set and enforce healthy boundaries in future relationships is crucial for preventing further manipulation and abuse.

Case Studies: Escaping the Sociopath

The following case studies highlight real or fictionalised examples of individuals who escaped toxic relationships with sociopaths and found a path to recovery.

Case Study 1: Sarah's Story

Sarah met her sociopathic partner, Alex, at a social event. He was charming, attentive, and seemed to have everything she was looking for in a partner. In the beginning, he showered her with affection, constantly telling her how special she was and making her feel like the centre of his world.

However, over time, Alex began to change. He started to criticise Sarah's appearance, her friends, and even her career. He became increasingly controlling, isolating her from her social circle and making her feel like she was incapable of making decisions on her own. Whenever Sarah tried to assert her independence, Alex would gaslight her, telling her she was being irrational or overreacting.

Despite the emotional abuse, Sarah found it difficult to leave the relationship. She had become emotionally attached to Alex and believed that his moments of kindness and affection were proof that he truly loved her. It wasn't until Sarah confided in a close friend that she realised the extent of the manipulation she had endured.

With the support of her friend and a therapist, Sarah eventually found the strength to leave Alex. The healing process was difficult, but over time, Sarah rebuilt her self-esteem and regained control of her life. She now uses her experience to help others recognise the signs of emotional abuse and find the courage to escape toxic relationships.

Case Study 2: Mark's Workplace Nightmare

Mark worked for a large corporation where he had a boss, Julia, who was highly regarded by upper management but created a toxic work environment for her employees. Julia would frequently take credit for Mark's work, undermine his

Contributions, and gaslight him when he tried to address the issues. She would praise him one day and tear him down the next, leaving him feeling confused and demoralized.

Mark's anxiety grew as he constantly worried about his job security and his performance. Julia manipulated office politics to turn Mark's colleagues against him, making him feel isolated and powerless.

After months of enduring this emotional abuse, Mark finally reached out to HR and began documenting Julia's behaviour. With the help of HR and supportive colleagues, Mark was able to confront the situation and eventually transfer to a different department, where he thrived in a healthier work environment.

Mark's experience highlights the impact of sociopathic behaviour in the workplace and the importance of standing up to emotional abuse.

In this chapter, we've explored the emotional and psychological toll that sociopaths have on their victims. Through emotional manipulation, gaslighting, and trauma bonding, sociopaths create a cycle of abuse that leaves their victims feeling helpless, confused, and deeply wounded. However, with recognition, support, and a commitment to healing, it is possible for victims to break free from these toxic relationships and reclaim their lives.

Chapter 8:

Protecting Yourself from Sociopaths

Sociopaths, with their charm, manipulation, and lack of empathy, can infiltrate every area of life—romantic relationships, friendships, workplaces, and even family settings. While it may not always be possible to avoid encountering a sociopath, it is absolutely possible to protect yourself from their harmful influence. This chapter is designed to help you recognise early signs, set boundaries, and take steps toward self-care and emotional recovery.

Setting Firm Boundaries

Sociopaths often test boundaries early in relationships, whether personal or professional. One of the best ways to protect yourself is by setting and maintaining firm boundaries. Boundaries are not just physical but also emotional, mental, and relational. Establishing clear lines about what behaviours are acceptable and what aren't helps prevent manipulation and exploitation.

Why Sociopaths Test Boundaries

Sociopaths thrive on manipulation, and to gain control over their victims, they first need to understand where the person's boundaries lie. They may test limits by making inappropriate comments, asking for favours that feel too much too soon, or pushing emotional boundaries to see how far they can go without being challenged. These small infractions may not seem significant at first but are red flags indicating that a larger violation of boundaries could be coming.

How to Establish Firm Boundaries

1. Know Your Limits: The first step to setting boundaries is being clear on what behaviours you are comfortable with and what is non-negotiable for you. These limits should be personal and reflect your own values and emotional needs.

2. Be Clear and Direct: When a sociopath crosses a boundary, respond with a clear and firm statement. For example, "I'm uncomfortable when you speak to me that way" or "I don't appreciate being treated like this."

3. Stand Your Ground: Sociopaths often respond to boundary-setting by trying to wear down the person. They might challenge your boundaries, dismiss your feelings, or try to guilt you into backing down. Staying consistent and firm is essential.

4. Non-Negotiable Boundaries: Identify which boundaries are absolute and non-negotiable, such as personal safety, respect, and honesty. If a sociopath crosses these boundaries, it's time to take serious action and consider ending the relationship, or at least distancing yourself.

5. Consequences for Boundary Violations: Boundaries are ineffective without consequences. If someone crosses your boundaries, make sure there is a consequence. This could mean stepping back from the relationship or limiting interactions to only necessary or formal settings.

What to Watch For

Sociopaths are skilled at testing boundaries slowly and subtly, making it harder to notice when they are gradually encroaching on your emotional or personal space. Be aware of the following:

- Pushing for too much too soon: Whether in relationships, friendships, or at work, a sociopath may try to accelerate the relationship unnaturally fast. This often includes excessive flattery, asking for significant favours early on, or demanding emotional closeness.

- Ignoring your discomfort: If you express discomfort or displeasure with something they've said or done, they may dismiss it or act like it's not a big deal.

- Using charm or manipulation: After pushing your boundaries, they might try to charm their way back into your good graces, making you second-guess your own feelings.

Recognizing When to Cut Ties

Not all sociopaths are easily avoided. Some may be family members, coworkers, or people with whom we share responsibilities. While cutting ties is often the healthiest option, it's not always possible or safe to do so immediately. However, recognising when a relationship has become toxic and taking steps to distance yourself is crucial for your emotional well-being.

When to Cut Ties

1. Repeated Boundary Violations: If someone continues to disrespect your boundaries despite repeated warnings, this is a clear sign that the relationship is unhealthy.

2. Gaslighting and Manipulation: If you find yourself constantly questioning your reality or feeling manipulated, these are signs of emotional abuse. Sociopaths often employ these tactics to maintain control.

3. Emotional and Psychological Drain: If a relationship leaves you feeling emotionally drained, anxious, or depressed more often than it brings you joy or fulfilment, it may be time to distance yourself.

4. Lack of Empathy and Exploitative Behaviour: Sociopaths frequently exploit others for their own gain, showing little to no empathy for the harm they cause. If you are consistently being taken advantage of or hurt by someone who shows no remorse, it's time to assess the relationship.

How to Cut Ties Safely

1. Create an Exit Plan: If you're dealing with a sociopath in a close relationship, such as a partner, friend, or family member, plan your exit carefully. Make sure you have the necessary support in place before taking action.

2. Minimise Contact: Reducing contact is the first step to cutting ties with a sociopath. This could mean limiting

conversations to only what is absolutely necessary or moving toward no contact if possible.

3. Set Firm Boundaries in Group Settings: If it's not possible to completely cut ties—such as with a sociopathic coworker or family member at gatherings—set strict boundaries. Limit your interactions to formal or group settings, and avoid engaging in personal conversations.

4. Document Abusive Behaviour: In some cases, particularly in work or legal contexts, it's important to keep a record of any manipulative, deceitful, or abusive behaviour. This can be essential if you need to report the person to HR or involve authorities.

Self-Care and Emotional Recovery

After dealing with a sociopath, self-care is vital. Sociopaths leave their victims emotionally exhausted, confused, and often riddled with self-doubt. Whether you've ended a toxic relationship or distanced yourself from a sociopathic influence, the road to recovery involves rebuilding your emotional strength and mental resilience.

The Importance of Therapy

Therapy plays a critical role in recovering from the emotional damage caused by sociopathic abuse. A skilled therapist can help you process your emotions, rebuild your self-esteem, and develop healthy coping mechanisms. Therapy can also help you work through any feelings of guilt, shame, or anger that may linger after your exposure to a sociopath.

- Cognitive Behavioural Therapy (CBT) can be particularly effective in helping victims of sociopathic abuse recognise and challenge distorted thinking patterns, such as self-blame or learned helplessness.

- Trauma-focused therapy is essential for those who have experienced deep emotional or psychological harm, especially if trauma bonding or long-term manipulation has occurred.

- Support Groups: Connecting with others who have experienced similar situations can also be helpful. Support groups provide validation, reduce feelings of isolation, and offer practical advice for healing.

Self-Reflection and Personal Growth

In addition to therapy, self-reflection is an important tool for healing. Reflecting on your experiences and gaining insight into the patterns of manipulation you encountered can help prevent similar situations in the future. Journaling or talking through your experiences with a trusted friend or therapist can help you make sense of the manipulation, deceit, and emotional abuse you endured.

Rebuilding Self-Esteem

Sociopaths often erode their victims' self-worth, leaving them feeling unworthy or incapable. A key aspect of recovery is rebuilding self-esteem and rediscovering your inner strength. Activities that promote personal growth, such as setting new goals, learning new skills, or engaging in hobbies that bring you joy, can help you regain confidence and a sense of self.

Mindfulness and Stress Reduction

Dealing with a sociopath can leave you feeling anxious and hyper vigilant, constantly on guard against manipulation or deceit. Mindfulness practices such as meditation, deep breathing exercises, and yoga can help you reduce anxiety and regain a sense of calm and control over your emotions.

Support Networks

A strong support network is essential when recovering from a relationship with a sociopath. Whether it's trusted friends, family members, or professional therapists, having people who understand your experience and can offer guidance and emotional support is key to your recovery.

Friends and Family

Lean on people who have your best interests at heart and who have demonstrated they can be trusted. Confide in those who will listen without judgment and who can provide a safe space for you to express your emotions. Sharing your experience can offer relief, and trusted friends or family members can help you see things more clearly if you're doubting yourself.

Therapists and Counsellors

A therapist can help guide you through the process of healing, offering tools and strategies to regain your emotional balance and self-confidence. They can also help you identify unhealthy patterns that might have been reinforced during your relationship with the sociopath and help you break free from those habits.

Support Groups

Joining a support group specifically for victims of sociopaths or emotional abuse can be incredibly validating. Hearing from others who have gone through similar experiences can help you feel less alone and provide practical advice on how to rebuild your life after escaping a sociopathic influence.

Interactive Section: Sociopathic Behaviour Checklist

To help you recognise sociopathic behaviour in your daily life, use the following checklist to assess whether someone in your life may be exhibiting sociopathic traits:

1. Charm and Charisma: Does the person seem excessively charming or charismatic, particularly when first meeting them?

2. Manipulation of Small Situations: Do they manipulate small events or interactions to their advantage, even if it seems unnecessary?

3. Pathological Lying: Have you caught them lying about things that seem trivial or unnecessary?

4. Lack of Empathy: Do they seem unable to genuinely understand or care about the feelings of others, especially in times of distress?

5. Excessive Flattery: Do they constantly flatter you in a way that feels excessive or insincere?

6. Exploitative Behaviour: Do they frequently take advantage of others, either by manipulating situations or using people to get what they want?

7. Gaslighting: Do they often make you doubt your memory, perception, or reality by denying events or twisting facts?

If you've answered "yes" to several of these questions, the person in your life may be exhibiting sociopathic traits. Consider consulting a therapist or trusted individual to discuss how to approach the situation safely and how to protect yourself moving forward.

Conclusion

Protecting yourself from sociopaths requires a combination of vigilance, firm boundaries, emotional resilience, and self-care. By recognising the signs of sociopathic behaviour early, setting clear limits, and seeking support when needed, you can safeguard your well-being and avoid becoming a victim of manipulation and emotional abuse. Remember, it's possible to regain control of your life and rebuild your emotional strength after exposure to a sociopath—your path to healing begins with self-awareness, support, and a commitment to self-care.

Conclusion: Protecting Yourself from Sociopaths and Moving Forward

Sociopathy is a complex and often misunderstood condition, one that affects not only those diagnosed with it but also the people around them. Sociopaths, with their charm, manipulative tendencies, and lack of empathy, can cause lasting emotional, psychological, and even physical harm to those who fall within their sphere of influence. Understanding sociopathy is the first step toward recognising the warning signs, protecting oneself, and fostering resilience in the face of such individuals.

In this conclusion, we will revisit the key points from the preceding chapters and reflect on the importance of being aware of sociopaths in our lives. More importantly, we will discuss how you can use this knowledge to move forward in a healthier, more empowered way.

Final Thoughts on Sociopathy

Sociopathy, as outlined throughout this book, represents a range of behaviours that can be destructive and manipulative. Sociopaths are often adept at blending into society, using charm, deceit, and psychological manipulation to get what they want from others without remorse or guilt. They may not always present as the dangerous individuals we see in popular media; many sociopaths are functioning members of society who exploit others for personal gain in more subtle, everyday ways.

We've explored the psychological underpinnings of sociopathy, its manifestations in various settings such as personal relationships and the workplace, and the tactics sociopaths use to remain undetected. From gaslighting to pathological lying, sociopaths have a toolbox of manipulative strategies that enable them to maintain control over their victims. Recognising these behaviours early on is crucial in avoiding or minimising harm.

The Role of Manipulation in Sociopathic Behaviour

A central theme that has emerged in the discussion of sociopathy is the way sociopaths manipulate others. Whether through charm, deceit, or the use of psychological tactics like gaslighting, sociopaths thrive on control. They lack empathy, which makes it easy for them to exploit the emotional vulnerabilities of their victims. One of the most dangerous aspects of sociopathy is that the manipulation is often so subtle that the victim may not even realise they are being controlled until significant damage has already been done.

Why Sociopaths Go Unnoticed

Sociopaths can be difficult to detect because they are often skilled at wearing a mask of normalcy or even likability. As we've discussed, sociopaths don't always fit the stereotype of the violent or overtly antisocial criminal. Instead, many sociopaths are charming, seemingly well-adjusted individuals who build superficial relationships that serve their own self-interest. They may excel in careers, particularly in environments where competition and a lack of empathy are seen as advantageous, such as corporate or political settings.

Despite their superficial charm and success, sociopaths leave a trail of emotional devastation in their wake. They may engage in emotional abuse, manipulation, gaslighting, and deception, gradually eroding the self-esteem and mental health of their victims. Yet, because they present so well to the outside world, their actions often go unnoticed or unchallenged.

 The Power of Awareness: Protecting Yourself from Sociopaths

One of the primary goals of this book has been to provide you with the tools to recognise the subtle and overt signs of sociopathy. Knowledge is your greatest defence against manipulation, and understanding how sociopaths operate allows you to take proactive steps to protect yourself. Whether in personal relationships, friendships, or professional environments, the strategies outlined in this book can help you build resilience and safeguard your emotional and mental well-being.

Empowering Yourself Through Knowledge

The first step in protecting yourself is acknowledging that sociopaths exist in all walks of life and that you have the power to guard yourself against their influence. By understanding the signs and behaviours associated with sociopathy, you can trust your instincts when something feels off in an interaction or relationship. Early detection of sociopathic behaviour can help you set boundaries, disengage from harmful individuals, and avoid becoming entangled in manipulative or abusive dynamics.

In earlier chapters, we explored specific signs that may indicate sociopathy, including charm and charisma, inconsistent stories, pathological lying, and lack of empathy. Recognising these traits allows you to evaluate whether someone in your life may be exhibiting sociopathic tendencies and take appropriate action to protect yourself.

Setting Boundaries

Sociopaths are notorious for testing boundaries. As we
discussed in Chapter 8, establishing and maintaining
firm boundaries is one of the most effective ways to
protect yourself. This means being clear about your
limits in both personal and professional relationships and
enforcing those limits consistently. Sociopaths will often
attempt to erode boundaries over time, using charm,
manipulation, or guilt to push past your defences. Being
vigilant and staying firm in your resolve is key to
preventing them from gaining control over your life.

Self-Care and Emotional Recovery

Exposure to a sociopath can take a significant toll on
your mental and emotional well-being. Victims of
sociopaths often experience self-doubt, anxiety,
depression, and trauma. Recognising the signs of
emotional and psychological abuse is crucial in the
healing process. Self-care, therapy, and surrounding
yourself with supportive individuals can help you
recover from the damage inflicted by a sociopath.

Healing is a gradual process, and there may be moments when you feel overwhelmed or unsure of how to move forward. This is where professional help, such as therapy, can be invaluable. A therapist can help you process your emotions, rebuild your self-esteem, and develop strategies for reclaiming control of your life after the harm caused by a sociopath.

Trusting Your Instincts

One of the most important takeaways from this book is the importance of trusting your instincts. Sociopaths are skilled at creating doubt and confusion in their victims, often leading people to question their own perceptions and feelings. If you find yourself in a relationship—whether personal, professional, or social—that feels wrong or leaves you feeling drained, anxious, or manipulated, trust that instinct. Often, our intuition picks up on subtle cues that we may not consciously recognise, alerting us to the danger of manipulative or harmful behaviour.

Learning to listen to and trust your inner voice is a powerful tool for protecting yourself from sociopaths. If something feels off, don't dismiss it. Take a step back, assess the situation, and evaluate whether the person you're dealing with is exhibiting signs of manipulative or sociopathic behaviour.

A Path Forward: Applying Your Knowledge in Daily Life

Now that you have a deeper understanding of sociopathy and the tactics sociopaths use to manipulate and exploit others, it's time to think about how you can apply this knowledge to your own life. Whether you suspect someone in your life may exhibit sociopathic tendencies or you're simply looking to protect yourself from potential harm, the strategies and insights shared in this book can guide you.

Evaluating Relationships

After reading this book, take some time to reflect on the relationships in your life. Are there individuals who frequently make you feel anxious, insecure, or manipulated? Do you find yourself questioning your own reality or feeling guilty for asserting your boundaries? If so, these may be signs of a toxic or manipulative relationship.

As you evaluate your relationships, consider whether the behaviours you've identified align with the signs of sociopathy we've discussed. It's important to be objective and fair in your assessment, but also trust your own feelings and observations.

Making Informed Decisions

Armed with the knowledge you've gained; you can now make more informed decisions about your relationships and interactions. If you believe someone in your life is a sociopath or exhibits sociopathic tendencies, you have the power to set boundaries, limit your interactions, or, if necessary, cut ties entirely. While it may not always be easy to distance yourself from a sociopath—especially if they are a family member or coworker—there are steps you can take to protect yourself.

Consider the strategies we discussed in earlier chapters for dealing with sociopaths in various settings. Whether in the workplace, in a romantic relationship, or in a family dynamic, there are practical steps you can take to minimise the influence of a sociopath and safeguard your emotional well-being.

Building Resilience

Dealing with sociopaths can leave you feeling drained and emotionally vulnerable, but it can also offer an opportunity for growth and resilience. By learning to recognise manipulation and setting clear boundaries, you become more resilient to harmful influences. Over time, you'll develop the confidence to protect yourself from toxic individuals and prioritise your own mental and emotional health.

Building resilience doesn't happen overnight, but with practice, you'll find that you're better equipped to handle difficult personalities and challenging relationships. Surround yourself with supportive individuals, engage in self-care practices, and continue to prioritise your well-being as you move forward.

Ending on a Positive Note: Trusting Your Instincts and Prioritising Well-Being

In closing, it's important to remember that while sociopaths can be highly manipulative and damaging, you have the power to protect yourself. By trusting your instincts, setting boundaries, and recognising the early signs of manipulation, you can prevent sociopaths from gaining control over your life. While it may take time and effort to extricate yourself from a toxic relationship or recover from the harm caused by a sociopath, it is entirely possible to rebuild your life, regain your self-esteem, and emerge stronger than before.

Prioritising Mental and Emotional Well-Being

Your mental and emotional well-being should always be your top priority. Dealing with difficult personalities— whether they are sociopaths or simply toxic individuals —requires a commitment to self-care and emotional balance. Prioritise your well-being by seeking therapy, engaging in activities that bring you joy, and surrounding yourself with supportive and caring individuals.

If you find yourself doubting your decisions or feeling uncertain about a relationship, take a step back and reassess the situation. Remember, your well-being comes first, and no relationship or interaction is worth sacrificing your mental health.

Trusting Yourself

Above all, trust yourself. Trust your instincts, your perceptions, and your ability to protect yourself from harm. Sociopaths thrive on creating doubt and confusion, but by staying grounded in your own truth and trusting your inner voice, you can navigate difficult relationships and avoid falling prey to manipulation.

Moving forward, use the knowledge you've gained in this book to make informed decisions, set boundaries, and prioritise your well-being. You have the power to protect yourself from sociopaths and to create a life that is free from manipulation and emotional abuse. Your journey toward healing and empowerment begins now.

Final Words

Sociopathy is a pervasive issue that affects countless individuals worldwide. While sociopaths may appear charming, competent, or even kind on the surface, their true nature often reveals itself over time through manipulation, deceit, and emotional abuse. By understanding the signs of sociopathy, recognising manipulative behaviours, and taking proactive steps to protect yourself, you can minimise the risk of harm and reclaim control over your life.

Remember that you are not alone in this journey. Support networks, therapy, and trusted friends and family members can help you navigate the complexities of dealing with sociopaths and provide you with the strength and encouragement you need to move forward.

Your well-being is worth protecting, and with the knowledge and tools gained from this book, you are better equipped than ever to safeguard your emotional health and build a brighter, healthier future.

www.ingramcontent.com/pod-product-compliance
Lightning Source LLC
Chambersburg PA
CBHW060516290526
45791CB00001B/405